T0077786

Treasures of My Life

AN INSPIRATIONAL COLLECTION OF POEMS AND ART

By Marcella Archibald

Thanks God

Feel the Healing, Embrace the Love.

Claim the Life You Were Meant To Live.

Order this book online at www.trafford.com
or email orders@trafford.com

Most Trafford titles are also available at major online book retailers.

Printed in the United States of America.

ISBN: 978-1-4251-6274-0 (sc)

Trafford rev. 01/29/2011

www.trafford.com

North America & international
toll-free: 1 888 232 4444 (USA & Canada)
phone: 250 383 6864 • fax: 812 355 4082

And His strength is in the clouds.

Psalm 68 – Pray 34

And he shall be like a tree planted by the rivers of water, that bringeth forth His fruit in his season: His leaf shall not wither and whatsoever he doeth shall prosper.

Psalm 1 – Pray 3

ACKNOWLEDGMENTS

Grateful Acknowledgment to my Son Nathaniel who has given his time, his technical skills and timeless support in bringing these wonderful works to be.
Devon thanks for the love.

To all the friends that have journeyed for the last four years with me. Thanks for the joy.

FOREWORD

Strength comes from within; courage comes with faith and belief. The result is true healing.

From my experience healing happens *when you have successfully believed that you can overcome your positions, events in your life and your circumstances.* It is marked by your connection with others. A gentle change takes place in and round about you, offering an opportunity to genuinely embrace the gifts that are offered.

My gift of healing was welcomed after what seemed to be a hopeless illness. It transformed a path that initially appeared to be leading to a dire outcome.

Richness in life was achieved. Consequently, *I was Divinely guided* to write these poems. Each line was drawn from my experience of hardship and my healing through a very complex journey.

The road traveled has been long and arduous with many challenges. With perseverance and steadfastness I braced the lessons that were put before me.

Spirit gave me the will to live and so I feel compelled to share my collection of poems with you. Through the words my story unfold to affirm that no matter what challenges may come about determination, gratitude and a keen motivation to survive will truly bring you to a place more rewarding than you could ever possibly imagine.

A RICH LIFE IS ACHIEVED WHEN WE CAN TAKE A MINUTE TO COUNT OUR BLESSINGS.

Marcella
October 2004

ARTS OF PURPOSE

1. SMILE – I shall yet praise Him who is the health of my countenance. PSALM 42-Pray 11.
2. SILENCE – Therefore let thy words be few – ECCLESIASTES 5 – Pray 2.
3. WHEN I WAS YOUNG – When I was a child I spake as a child – 1 CORINTHIANS 13 – Pray 11.
4. TO A MOTHERS SON – And when she saw him that he was a goodly child – EXODUS 2 – Pray 2.
5. GRACE – Your speech be always with grace – COLOSSIANS 4 – Pray 6
6. RISE TO THE NEW DAY – His compassions fail not. They are new every morning. LAMENTATIONS 3 – Pray 22-23.
7. THE WALK – to walk in all His ways, and to love Him. DEUTERONOMY 10 – Pray 12.
8. THE JOURNEY – and by my God have I leaped over a wall. PSALM 18 – Pray 29.
9. FLOWERS – and His flowers, were of the same. EXODUS 37 – Pray 17.
10. ANGEL – And the angel that talked with me – ZACHARIAS 1 – Pray 9.
11. YAWN – If they shall enter into my rest. HEBREWS 4 – Pray 5.
12. COCOON – In all things we are more than conquerors through Him that loved us. ROMANS 8 – Pray 37.
13. BLESSINGS – And all these blessings shall come on thee – DEUTERONOMY 28 – Pray 2.
14. HEAVEN'S LIGHT – In Thy light shall we see light – PSALM 36 – Pray 9.
15. TEARS – With Joy shall ye draw water out of the wells of salvation. ISAIAH 12 – Pray 3.
16. JOY – And your Joy no man taketh from you. SAINT-JOHN 16 – Pray 22.

17. AWAKENING – Arise, shine for Thy Light is come. ISAIAH 60 – Pray 1.
18. FIRST STEP – that ye should follow his steps. 1 PETER 2 – Pray 21.
19. ROSE – I Am the rose of Sharon. SOLOMON 2 – Pray 1.
20. FRIEND – A man that hath friends must shew himself friendly. PROVERBS 18 – Pray 24.
21. PAIN – for I have learned, whatsoever state I am, therewith to be content. PHILIPPIANS 6 – Pray 11.
22. WISDOM – and the sword of the Spirit, which is the Word of God. EPHESIANS 6 – Pray 17.
23. THE TOUCH – Saying, Touch not my anointed. PSALM 105 – Pray 15.
24. SONG OF PRAISE – Make a joyful noise unto The Lord. PSALM 100 – Pray 1.
25. SADNESS – but we glory in tribulations also. ROMANS 5 – Pray 3.
26. CREATIVITY – nothing better, than that a man should rejoice in his own works. ECCLESIASTES 3 – Pray 22.
27. LAUGHTER – Then was our mouth filled with laughter. PSALM 126 – Pray 2.
28. LIFE – To him that overcometh will I give to eat of the tree of life. REVELATION 2 – Pray 7.
    For there is hope of a tree. JOB 14 – Pray 7.
29. SPIRIT – Thou sendest forth Thy Spirit, they are created. PSALM 104 – Pray 30.
30. THE VOICE WITHIN – The voice of The Lord is powerful –PSALM 29 – Pray 4.

WHEN MAN HAS MADE PERFECT THE LOVE OF GOD WITHIN—THEN CAN MAN SEE THE BEAUTY OF ALL THINGS.

CONTENTS

SMILE

Today a smile came on my face
It found its way to me
It came from some far off place
Why it came is somewhat of a mystery

I welcomed the smile that came to be
like any good guest I gave the best of me
I let it stay on my face awhile
So good to have its company

Like any good host I embraced the smile
became raptured in its charm
No questions asked, no thoughts about
It was entertained with warmth

Though I know my guest will leave
Somehow it knew my needs
It's nice to have this pleasantness
When the moments look so bleak

Oh smile, oh smile, a treasure to behold
So glad you came, no longer kept at bay
The mystery as to why you came is slowly drifting away
Oh so glad you took a chance and called on me today

SILENCE

A fallen leaf
Shadows on the wall
Mirrored self

Lost Time

Inward thoughts
Streams of light
Ray of hope

A Crescendo

Unmeasured sleep
Untangled dreams
Colours of solitude

Patterns of Life

WHEN I WAS YOUNG

When I was young
I laughed a lot
And tripped along the beach
I can still feel the rolling waves
Splashing at my feet

When I Was Young
I danced a lot
Life was my rhythmic beat
I can still hear the melodies from so long ago
Music oh so sweet

When I Was Young
I played a lot
Oh so excessively
I can still close my eyes and see myself
Joyous as can be

When I Was Young
I dreamt a lot
Countless thoughts, unable to describe
I can still touch my heart, and recall
The moments with great pride

TO A MOTHER'S SON

So proud you are my son
I constantly beam with pride
images fondly cross my mind
happiness gently stirs warmth inside

You bring unconditional joy to me each passing day
Others I'm sure too will confess
Your magnetic natural way of being
Peaceful, reverence, devotion to kindness

I watched you grow from year to year
With ease and form, maturity took stride
Proudly I know stand aside
Acclaim, enjoy, embrace, celebrate the child

As you continue on life's journey
May all your experiences give you wisdom
May all your failures give you strength
May all your friendships give you countless memories
Create your tomorrows with today's dreams

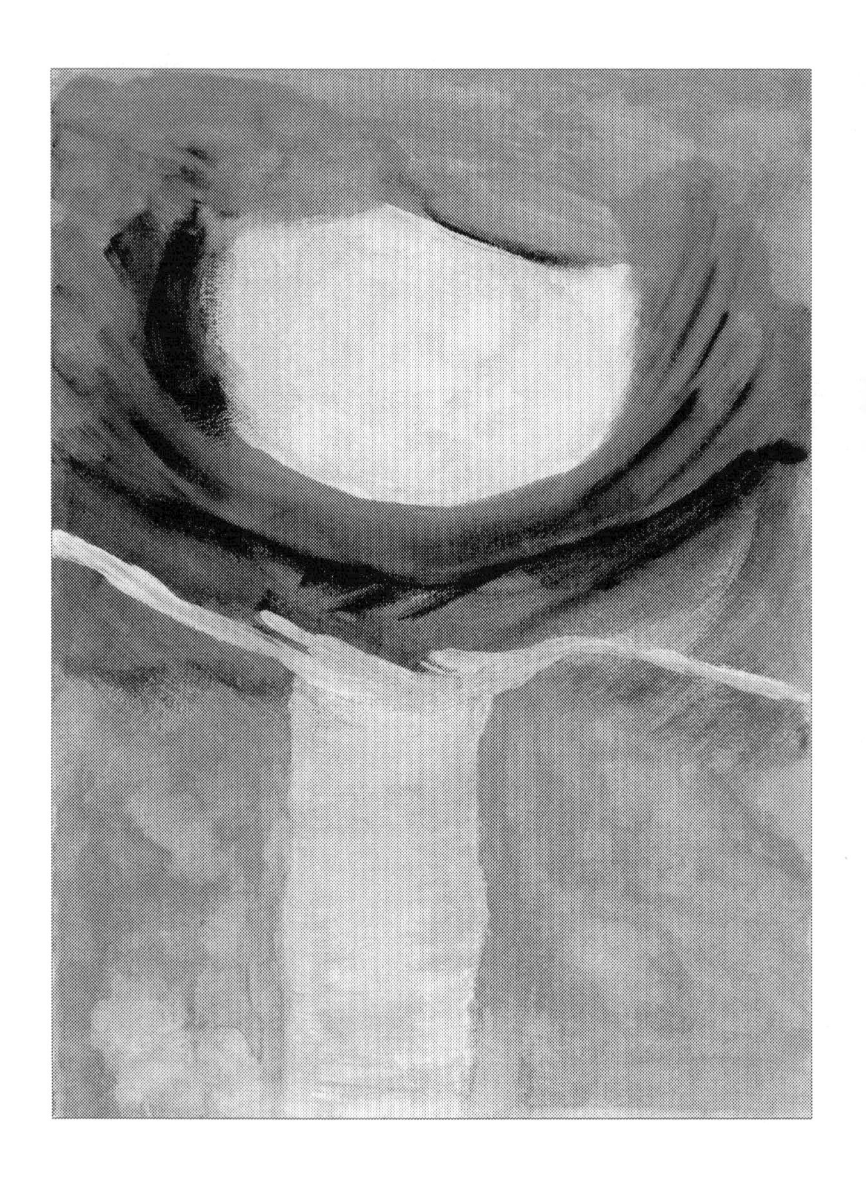

RISE TO THE NEW DAY

Amidst the slanted rays
Morning filters though the windowpane
What will it reveal to day
How joyful, How compelling
Rise To The New Day

Whatever chartered course
Render yourself to the unknown
What will I succumb to to day
How blinded, How uninspired

Rise To The New Day

Like footprints in the sand
Images, impressions are stamped
What's the New Day magic
How timeless, How unrevealing

Rise To The New Day

As the day beckons onward
Hopes, dreams , pleasures, passengers of time
What will be remembered
How soulful, How versed

Rise To The New Day

THE WALK

With abated breath I took a walk
Along life's corridor
Each turn I found an opportunity
Larger than the one before

With whispers and sighs
I forged on with gallant pride
Life's rhythm must be achieved
Keep the pace not to be deceived

A moment a thought goes fleeting by
Faded in the mosaic of the perceptive eye
Continued endurance must prevail
Opportunity comes not to the meek and the frail

Walk Tall, Walk Stout, Walk Strong
Continue the journey till success is won
With abated breath I walk no more
Along life's colourful corridor

I take the walk more leisurely
No longer with uncertainty
Question less as to what I see
Composed, Content, Humility

THE JOURNEY

I walked the earth so many days alone
My heart was there but my soul was stone
This entity has overtaken me
My Lord, My Jesus, Be Not Far From Me

My soul lay crumpled in some far off place
I had none to call upon, but my Faith
Months and seasons went drifting by
My Lord, My Jesus, Have You Heard My Cry?

Lift up your voice and call to Me
Your soul is not lost to eternity
Words from the heart are heard in prayers
My Lord, My Jesus, I Hold You So Dear

The day has come to take your claim
Remove from bondage and break the chain
Spiritual words will be your guide
My Lord, My Jesus, My Father On High

My Lord, My Lord I'm completely healed
Words uttered inside my heart, I Do Believe
Once again my soul is at peace,
I walk the path of truth, upright and with ease
My Lord, My Jesus, Always On My Side

Flowers
2004

FLOWERS

Kaleidoscope of Colours
Crescendo of Scents
Rhythmic Cascade

Embrace Me
Dazzle Me
Transform Me

Sunburst, Radiance, Rainbow
Intoxicating Sweetness
Exciting, Mysterious, Pure

Embrace Me
Dazzle Me
Transform Me

Natural treasure
Cupped, Captivating, Compelling
Frothing with luster

Embrace Me
Dazzle Me
Transform Me

YAWN

So simple, unrespected but yet so dear
I looked into my mirror and what did appear
A Yawn so sweet, it brought a twinkle to my eye
I let it rest on my face, oh for a little while

With great wonder and enormous glee
I let the Yawn enrapture me
So little I've seen of you these days
The time has come, to come out and play

Disappear not, be never far from me
I truly love to have your company
Reassurance, Comfort and Liberty
This is what my Yawn means to me

COCOON

Nestled in my cocoon of loneliness
Faded emotions, countless silence
Only The Wind On My Face

Inner thoughts, speak in magnitude
Timeless dreams, passing time
Only The Wind On My Face

Forgotten words, broken memories
Sincere reverence, determined mind
Only The Wind On My Face

Untranslated moments, emotional tapestry
Forge onward, brace the journey
Only The Wind On My Face

Silent applause, patterns of hope
Scattered rays, unmentionable colours

Only The Wind On My Face

BLESSINGS

A Basketful of Blessings
I receive each day
A Basketful of Blessings,
Each time I Pray

I didn't look far,
I didn't search high
A Basketful of Blessings,
Nothing to Buy

A Basketful of Blessings,
You ask
How can that be?
Look around you to day and
You will truly See

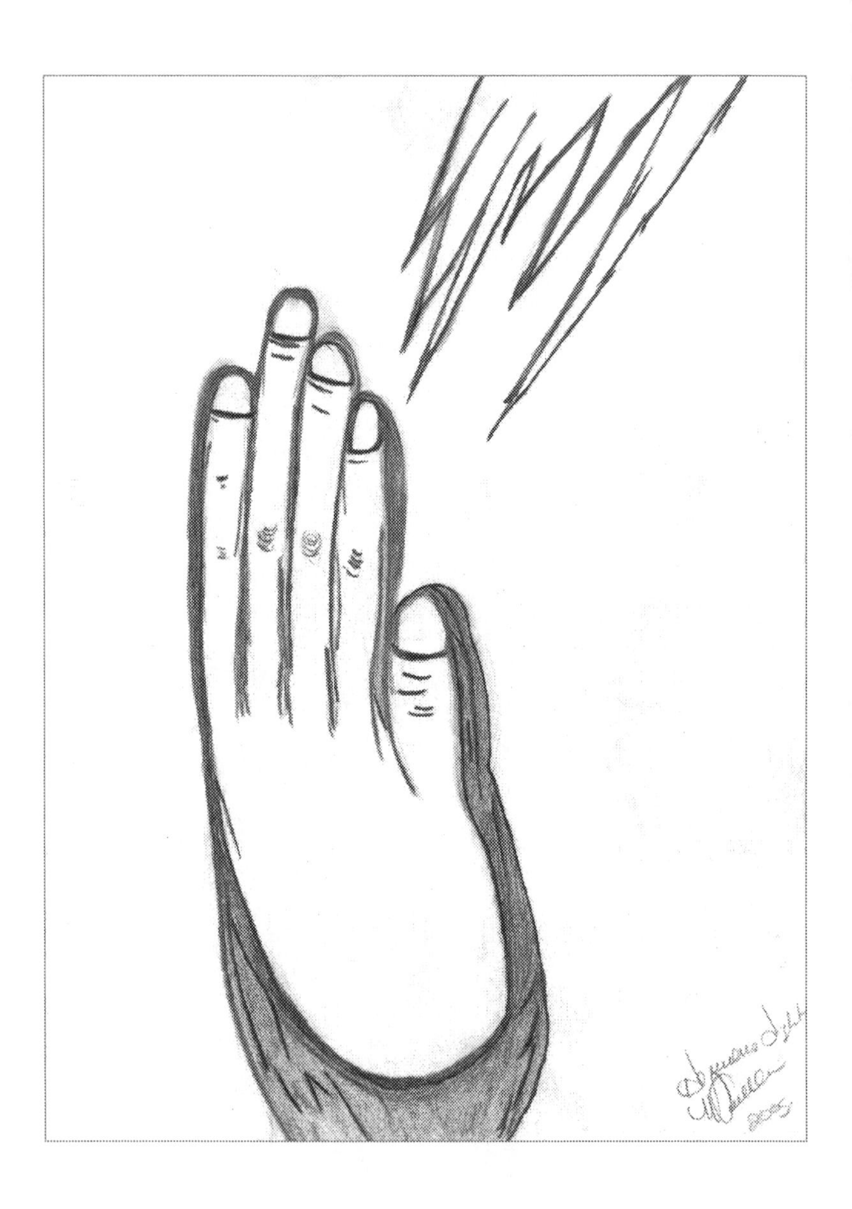

HEAVEN'S LIGHT

I caught myself leaving to day
I cried out to the Lord,
He Told Me – Just Pray

I grasped at the first words that came to me
I silently whispered out loud,
Lord, Not To day Please

The light was my beacon
A light I thought-not yet to see
I reached out to the Lord,
He Answered Me

I'm here to day because of his love for me
He opened my eyes that I might see
I'll always remember,
His Words To Me – Just Pray

TEARS

Invisible droplets
Soulful Symphony

Tears

Countless Emotions
Misty eyed

Tears

Calling on Sorrows
Explanation Shallow

Tears

Remembered Dreams
Borrowed Time

Tears

Succumb to Peace
Hold steadfast – Head Strong

Tears

JOY

Symphony of Love

Poetic Rhythm

Cascading colours

Emotional Peace

——

Dawn Awakened

Silent Prayer

Voices of Hope

Gentle embrace

——

Words of compassion

Patterns of Faith

Silent explanations

Unconditional Love

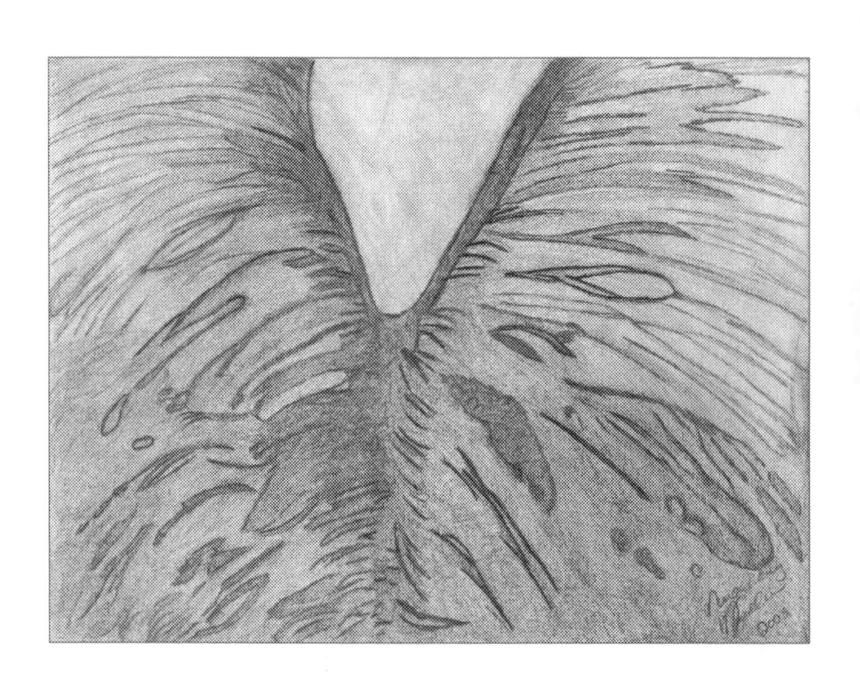

AWAKENING

A Wake Up Call I Received Today
All my doubts were taken away
A Miracle came my way that I may see
Believe In The Lord, He Will Set You Free

My Soul Was Lost, I Was Treated Unkind
His actions showed me, I was not left behind
A Miracle came my way that I may see
Believe In The Lord, He Will Set You Free

Awaken My Heart, Beat Gentle, Beat Strong
Embrace Life, the battle has been won
A Miracle came my way that I may see
Believe In The Lord, He Will Set You Free

FIRST STEP

I wanted to take a walk each day
Each step I made took my breath away
Succumb not to fear, soldier on
Journeys are not only for the strong

I took each step so gallantly
Step by step, gave strength to me
Succumb not to my foolish pride
My heart knew more – success on my side

Bravely walked the uncharted course
As the four seasons rolled into one
Succumb not to solitude – this too to be won
The journey oh so lonely – my heart without a song

I now walk the course more readily
Beauty abound, stupendously
Succumb to life – majestically
Remember the first step is humility

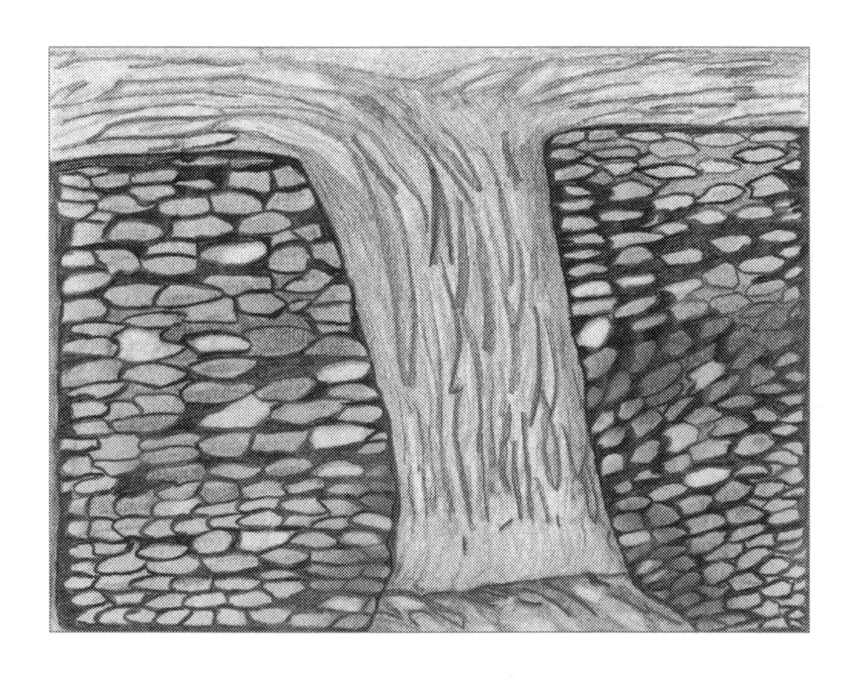

PAIN

Afflictions
Pented Emotions
A window into your heart

Clouded oppression
A look into your soul
Transparency

Untouched memories
A ribbon of unspoken words
Surrender

Silent submission
A countless moment

WISDOM

An Unspoken Word
A Silent Prayer
A Thought You Hold
A Calming Prayer

Earned Serenity
Tranquil Complacency
Inward Tranquility
Faith, Humbly, Peace
Honesty

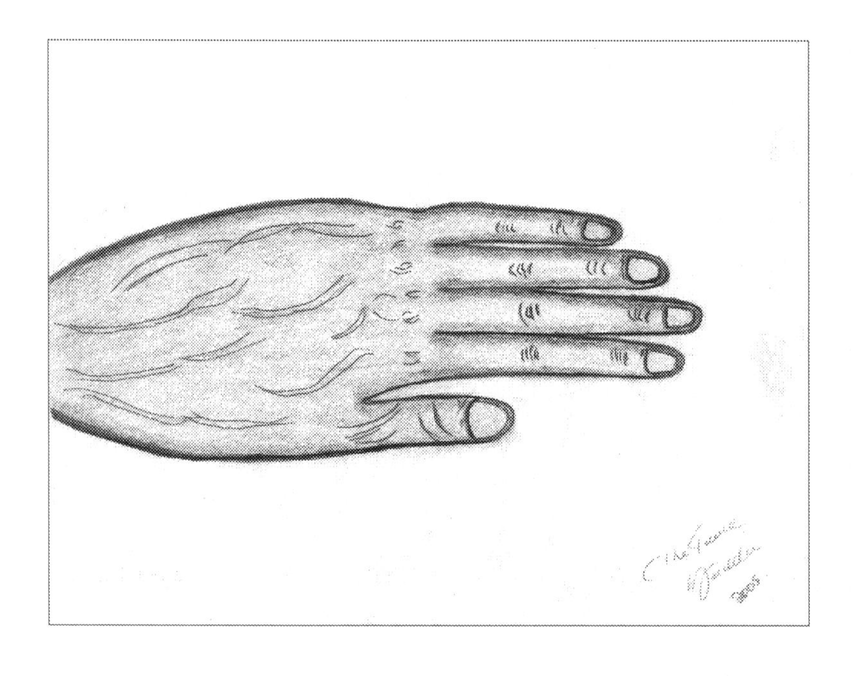

SONG OF PRAISE

Sing a Song
of Praise
My heart echoed clear

Melodies
Unsung
No practice run

Silently
Steadily
It whispered to me

Without Stage,
Print or Form
A comfort in the storm

Sing a Song
of Praise
My heart echoed clear

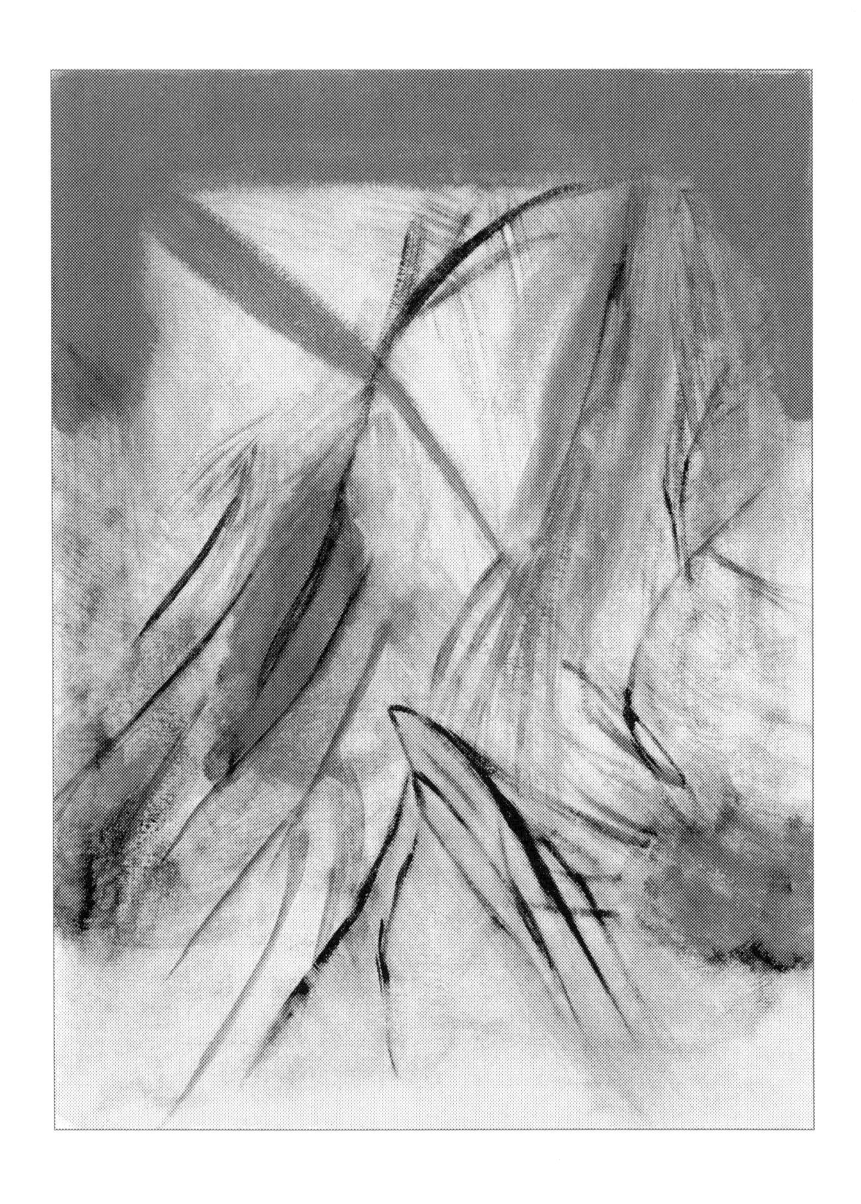

SADNESS

Like Sand dunes
The layers of life
Lay placidly on my soul

A whisper, a breath, a sigh
Twilight, dawn
Will it disappear

Softly twirling
Lapping against my heart
Conceded sorrows

Patterns of emotions
Etched deeply
Silently waiting to be erased

LAUGHTER

Like an underground spring
Rising and falling
Transparent
Contagious
Depth
Endless boundary

High-spirited melodies of tunes
Rising and falling
Echoes
Ascending
Resonating
Volume
Triumph insurmountable

Majestic beauty abound, created by life
Rising and falling
Multidimensional
Captivating
Emotions
Original always, lending itself to the moment

The Wall

LIFE

A timeless journey
Encompassed with exposure
Situations, experiences

Like a weathered note book
Chapters not yet recounted
Central to all living things

A rhythmic plain beckoning onwards
Beating out its own tempo
Succumbing to nothing

Strengthened by the marching of time
Shapeless beauty, mirrored attractions
Sensational splendour, universal gift

Spirit 2004

THE VOICE WITHIN

A whisper I heard, could it be
From some far off place it came to me
I knew not from whence it came
Truly This Thought Must Be Entertained

Quiet time it spent with me
Unburdened my heart
My soul it set free
Softly, Gently It Comforted Me

Silent words flow over me
I listened so attentively
Presence has overtaken me
Delicate, Complete, Delivery

AUTHOR'S NOTE

I am blest…

Through the course of my affliction my day to day desire was to triumph. With gladness I anchored on to the voice within, the guidance and direction of my creator. When no other gave knowledge or substance to my plight, I yield in full trust to the free love – depth unknown.

Blest with **Divine Guidance** I learned to pray, **JUST FOR TO DAY** – to seek Jesus for all my needs. **I to day rejoice**.

This day I have sound understanding life is a journey. The victory, to overcome all negativity with love, grace, belief, trust, strength, and joy.

Receive your basketful of blessings everyday with gratitude and humility.

My journey, I continue to have the pleasure and privilege to walk with Christ Jesus. His great love, joy, has been an fulfilling amazing and overflowing awakening.

This day my life is filled with great peace and an abundance of love by knowing and loving God. Surrendering all to the **Almighty** without doubt – hindrances – provocations. I can affirm this day – always touched by the will of God – all works – words – thoughts – deeds can be transformed and *blossom into healing.*

The **Power Of God** is at work in my life and those who I love and care for. I lay claim to the talents gifts – favors I receive with great zeal and an abundance of joy. Heart and love to day shall beckon you to seek only that which is for your *highest goodness.*

Keep in remembrance **the fullness of joy** – comes from within. **The love of God** is immeasurable and His treasures to us surpass all understanding. To day is a new day, an opportunity to do and embrace goodness.

Let the **love and beauty** of God be ***magnified*** in your life.

PURE LOVE IS THE GIFT OF GOD

Marcella
November 2007

TESTIMONIALS

Being part of Marcella's spiritual journey and the grateful recipient of her generous sharing of this journey with me has been and continues to be an incredibly moving and joyous experience. She has helped and continues to help me in my (sometimes faltering) steps towards living a life of Faith, Joy and Gratitude to God. I have no doubt that reading her book will be an inspiring and heartwarming experience. May God bless my dear friend in this path she is following in her life.
Mrs Kausalya Lokanathan

I have known Marcella for over three decades and I can truly attest to the remarkable turn of events in her personal life over the last few years. The things that have occurred have been such that she herself could not have brought them about nor would she have caused them to happen even were it possible because many involved health issues that she would have preferred to by-pass. Thus there is no other explanation for them except to say that there was a *Divine Intervention* in her life – resulting in an inner spiritual awakening that continues to the day and which has benefited herself – her family and many others. It is her desire that the present volume would be an extension of that benefit to others she may never personally meet, but who are searching and longing for an encounter with the God of the universe, who desire an *intimate relationship* with each of those He has created. It is to this end and under the guidance of The Holy Spirit she is publishing this book.
Sincerely, Carole Huggins
Montreal, November 2007

My dear friend Marcella, whom I've known for four decades, reentered my life March 2006. During her seven week stay at my home I learned that through Divine Intervention Marcella

survived a life threatening affliction that had changed her life forever. Marcella was truly a Miracle. After the affliction and as a result of this, I witnessed that she had the gift of writing inspirational poems, the hands to sketch artwork, and the ability to receive *Divine guidance*. I was in Awe. Marcella was Living Proof the True meaning of being one in *The Christ Mind* for her life was now devoted to prayer and helping others – doing God's work. To know Marcella is to experience wisdom, unconditional love, joy and peace. My husband and I are truly blest having Marcella in our lives, and we are grateful for we were given the opportunity through Marcella to embrace Christ Jesus. By Divine Guidance received – our lives are now being refashioned through daily prayer, giving thanks and doing our good works. Our lives are moving onward with great ease and now have purpose. To day I thank Jesus for saving Marcella's soul and giving her the opportunity to touch and change other souls through her many gifts.
Thank you my dear friend friend Marcella for all the prayers and wonderful guidance. God Bless you Marcella.
Journey on…
Noreen Smith
Vancouver, November 2007

FRIEND
We truly never know how we will be touched, here is one such soul, she struggled with near death experience only to be blessed with inspiration. Maybe it was always there deep down beneath the everyday rituals, the family needs, the long work hours that kept her running, until it all came to a halt. Time can be foe or friend! Luckily it was a friend.

Through affliction came light and the light is shared.

I applaud you: Louisa C.

"In times of great darkness and with no light when only one small candle is lit, the light of that small candle serves the same purpose and has the same effect as many high powered light bulbs. The small candle which was lit for me was Marcella and in times of great darkness when everything else had failed that small candle was my guiding light."
November 18, 2007
JL

I want to thank Marcella for having made God and Jesus Christ part of my every day life. In fact, since I met Marcella, I learned how to pray to God, through his Son Jesus Christ, his angels, archangels and other beings of the heavenly world. Almost every morning as I get up in the morning I give thanks to God for another day (especially on sunny days). Since I met Marcella, I learned to appreciate that we all go through good times and bad times in life, however, we must cherish the good times and enjoy the happy moments but to overcome the bad times and if we don't, worse things could happen. Sometimes it's hard to see the bright side of things when things don't go the way we expected them to go but by praying to God and asking God through his Son Jesus Christ to intervene sometimes we can overcome mountains – I have seen results coming right in front of my eyes and when I didn't get exactly what I asked for, I got something similar. I do not despair any more and I know God is there to help us and guide us when we call on him and I believe in God now more than ever. Thank you.
November 18, 2007
PD

My time with Marcella has been an amazing experience of the love, passion and sharing of TRUTH that has truly inspired my soul. Her faith and experience of the power and love of God

has been a blessing in my life. I have loved our time together and am witness of how the Spirit of our Lord is ever present in every step she takes. Anyone that meets God through her can see and feel the true healing power of how real love manifests in a pure heart. Thank you for your journey of peace. God bless you. I love you, Tania
Tania Fierro, BA, PCCT, MA

Blessed am I Jessica, to have had the opportunity to have met Marcella. Such joy and comfort our experience when engaging with Marcella, for she is one with Christ, delivering messages from The Source.
She shared with me the story of her transformation; she spoke of the beauty, the joy, the abundance of love that is experienced when we journey with God, with Christ Jesus.
Through the words of love, of inspiration, my heart opened to God, to Jesus. I now have also witnessed great change in my life, in my daughter's life.
Thank you Marcella
Praise God
Jessica
Vancouver

A new pathway… Ah, Marcella. With some trepidation we embarked on a new journey, recognizing that a morphing was taking place; That we are a work in progress, and not a finished product discovering our inner self and dimensions we hadn't quite known we were manifesting or about to become.
David
Vancouver

Hi Marcella
Engouragement is oxygen for the soul and you have definitely been an inspiration and motivation to me during these four

weeks' – Thank you for all of your kind words and gestures. I will always remember and pray for you. I hope you will continue to be a ray of light and hope in other peoples' lives.
God bless you!!!
Andrew W.
Tortolla – British Virgin Islands

To Marcella
People may say that this is a chance meeting – but I do understand that the meeting of our lives was by design and your sphere of influence has been widened forever. Your inner conviction comes through so loud and clear that my life has been changed forever.

I now truly know that living the life by the Word of God is the only way. My new quest is to let as much people as possible understand this. As for me the Inner Peace and joy as a result surpasses all treasures here on earth.
Love Learie
Ontario

Dearest Marcella
Thank you so much for your spiritual guidance. You are truly an inspiration. You have given me the insight to change the path of my Journey. Following the Christ like way, you have guided me to remove negativity and restore joy in my life. Thank you so much. May God continue to bless you and your family and may you continue helping others.
Love you
Bernadine
Ontario

Faithful seeker of the Divine truth and light
Lover of Jesus, His Love you bring to sight

His words of Love and guidance you speak
Reminding all in Jesus, we must believe and seek

A friend in deed though near or far
A sister in Christ, a shining star
A ray of sunshine on a cloudy day
In my heart you shall always stay.

May God continue to pour his blessings upon you and may you guide many souls into the Heavenly Kingdom.
In the name of Our Lord Jesus Christ.

With Love,
Lucia

You did it…

The words and images contained in this book represent so much more than can ever be conveyed to those that will partake of it.

A testament to your unfettered strength, courage and faith in overcoming obstacles that would break the spirit of man.

An intimate dialogue on the pleasures and pains of life.

Your Life.

Educating, uplifting, and renewing the spirits of those in need of guidance.

May this book, an affirmation to the fruits of your labours, nourish the minds, bodies, and souls of all those in need.

…Congratulations
Nathaniel

My Journey…

Journey On…

Journey On…

Journey On…

Journey On…

Journey On…

THE JOURNEY CONTINUES...